Where are You, Susie Petschek?

SUSIE PETSCHEK NERDESİN?

Cevat Çapan

Where are You, Susie Petschek?

SUSIE PETSCHEK NERDESİN?

❖

Translated by Cevat Çapan
& Michael Hulse
Introduced by A.S. Byatt

Arc
PUBLICATIONS
2001

Published by Arc Publications
Nanholme Mill, Shaw Wood Road
Todmorden, Lancs. OL14 6DA

Poems © Cevat Çapan 2001
Translation © Cevat Çapan and Michael Hulse 2001
Introduction © A.S. Byatt 2001

Design by Tony Ward
Printed at the Arc & Throstle Press
Nanholme Mill, Todmorden, Lancs.

ISBN 1 900072 43 2

The Publishers acknowledge financial assistance
from The Arts Council of England

Arc Publications: Visible Poet Series
Editor: Jean Boase-Beier

CONTENTS

Translator's preface / 9
Introduction / 13

PL
248
C36A233
2001

SERIES EDITOR'S NOTE

There is a prevailing view of translated poetry, especially in England, which maintains that it should read as though it had originally been written in English. The books in the *Visible Poets* series aim to challenge that view. They assume that the reader of poetry is by definition someone who wants to experience the strange, the unusual, the new, the foreign, someone who delights in the stretching and distortion of language which makes any poetry, translated or not, alive and distinctive. The translators of the poets in this series aim not to hide but to reveal the original, to make it visible and, in so doing, to render visible the translator's task, too. The reader is invited not only to experience the unique fusion of the creative talents of poet and translator embodied in the English poems in these collections, but also to speculate on the processes of their creation and so to gain a deeper understanding and enjoyment of both original and translated poems.

Jean Boase-Beier

TRANSLATOR'S PREFACE

To stroll down one of Istanbul's busy streets with Cevat Çapan, especially in that part of the city that was once the centre of the western European community and is now home to boutiques and bookshops and restaurants and consulates and galleries, is an enterprise that tends to require some time. Friends stop him every fifty yards to exchange the time of day. This one is a poet, that one a professor, the other runs the city's film festival: Cevat knows them all. Istanbul is his village. But a year or so ago it seemed to me that things had got a little out of hand. Total strangers would plant themselves in front of him and, beaming like long-lost friends, declare with emphasis "*You are Cevat Çapan!*" and enfold him in a mighty bear-hug. Cevat, smiling with an amiable mixture of modesty and gratification, enjoyed the show hugely and explained to me that a TV soap had recently run a sub-plot in which two teenagers interested in publishing careers had sought the avuncular advice of an established writer and publisher. Cevat had played himself for a number of episodes, till the sub-plot expired, and ever since had been contending with a kind of fame rarely granted to poets, as viewers not otherwise acquainted with his work complimented him on his acting skills and his kindness to the young.

It was in 1993, and thanks to the British Council, that I first met Cevat Çapan (pronounced Jévat Chapán). That May the Council flew to Istanbul three writers from the UK (Carol Ann Duffy, Michèle Roberts wearing her poet's hat, and myself) and Susan Bassnett of Warwick University (who takes an academic interest in translation). There we spent the better part of a week translating poetry with a number of Turkish poets as well as academics from universities in Istanbul, Ankara, Izmir and elsewhere. Educated Turks know French – frequently it is still the first foreign language for the Stamboul cosmopolitan, as Paris remains for many the principal point of western European orientation – but they know English too, and the Turkish versions of our poems which the participants produced were informed by real knowledge of our language, culture and literature; indeed, one of the poets present was Can Yücel (who died in 1999), among whose many achievements were outstanding translations of Dickinson, Eliot, Auden, and Dylan Thomas, as well as a number of Shakespeare's plays. We islanders, by contrast, had no Turkish and could bring little more than spirit to our reworkings of the prose literals we were provided with; but that we brought.

Between Cevat and myself there was an immediate rapport, and it was not too difficult – since Cevat is himself an experienced translator with a large sense of the tolerances that may assist a poem's passage – to negotiate an English for his poetry that was not too painfully snagged on the barbs of obstructive literalism. The poem that appears here as 'The Fire' was a product of that British Council workshop, and for those who have the Turkish it will be instructive to know that this rendering, though rich in liberties (beginning with the title), had Cevat's explicit blessing. Producing versions based on word-for-word cribs (supplied by Cevat himself throughout the years this book was in the making, with two or three by his wife Gönül in the early phase) has self-evident drawbacks: a translator not conversant with the language of the original runs serious risks of mistaking tone, register, rhythm, cultural and poetic subtext, and much more. Of course we attempted to counter these risks. At our irregular meetings in Istanbul over the last few years, we would spend hours on end in a variety of rooms – in his home, in a bookshop, in the offices of Adam (the publishing house where he is an editor), in the conference room of a business friend – immersed in the taxing affair of translation; and Cevat, as he drafted his literals, would pause at intervals to explain a personal or cultural or historical context, to gloss the connotations of individual words, to read out lines or whole poems so that I might hear the cadences of the original, and so forth. A computer at the Adam office almost reduced me to tears, for the characters on a Turkish keyboard were in such very different places from any I was familiar with that the keying of a single line took minutes; but otherwise we managed without impediment. With the generosity that is one of his salient characteristics, Cevat unfailingly applauded my English versions, while I for my part felt and still feel embarrassed by a sense that it was he who had done by far the larger part of the work; Cevat studied at Cambridge, his English is impeccable, and whenever the reader takes pleasure in the versions in this book, it is only fair to say that that is very nearly the pleasure of a direct rather than a mediated encounter.

Over the years of those intermittent visits to Istanbul, I have come to know Cevat Çapan the man well enough to savour deeply his friendship and that of his witty and quixotic wife Gönül and their three (adult) children. The writer who wears his learning lightly in his poems; who is intimate with the literature of many cultures and has given considerable thought to literature's place in the personal, social and political life of an individual; who loves his country, its ways and traditions, its people and places, but without making the provincial's mistake of taking one country for the world – this is the Cevat Çapan I have got to know. Like so many in Istanbul, he originally comes from Anatolia, and a down-to-earth straightforwardness of manner which I think has something of country ways in it remains in him, touching every aspect of his conduct, from the unaffected modesty with which he speaks (if pressed) of his own accomplishments, to the pleasure he takes in seeing a friend enjoy a well-prepared Turkish meal or in introducing him to the country's traditional music. At the same time, the great city's ease with the wider world has long since become second nature with him as well, and a spirit perhaps best described as pan-European is apparent in many of his cultural and publishing ventures and his own practice as teacher and translator (a spirit which of course includes engagement with poets from beyond Europe, from Neruda to Murray to Ashbery).

It is a tribute of sorts to Cevat Çapan, and also to the shaping influence of that remarkable city, Istanbul, if I confess to feeling uncertain whether to stress the internationalist in him or the man rooted in his own country. As the poems in this book show, the two sides are in fact seamlessly joined. It need only be said that, whatever the importance to him of Dostoyevsky, Akhmatova and Mandelstam, of Wittgenstein, Benjamin and Berger, there is a Cevat Çapan who always quickens to olive groves, the scent of pine and thyme, the thought of Lake Van, and the subtle velvet of Turkish well and sensitively used. "My life," he writes here, "has served to give beautiful names to my children." These poems too, though shorn of the beauty of their original sounds, are his children.

Michael Hulse 2001

The poems of Cevat Çapan are in many ways paradoxical. They sound ancient and traditional, and yet they are recognisably related to modernism. They are rooted in Turkish life and literature and yet they are European, and beyond that, aware of a world literature which means something, and in which they have a place. They are personal, concerned with his own family, his father's story, the names of his children, and yet they have the impersonality of old stories and tales. Çapan is a man obsessed by poetry, by literature, who has made his life from it, translating poets and playwrights from many languages, across many languages, yet his voice is his own and not 'literary'.

He has been my friend since we were at university together, in Cambridge at the end of the 1950s. He began writing his own poetry relatively late. I don't speak any Turkish, but I have listened to him reciting Nazim Hikmet and Oktay Rifat and many others, and I can therefore hear the ghost of the rhythms of his own work in his own language. He describes Turkish literature with passion and he seems to know everything else too. He was good for the insular undergraduate I was, and he still brings new things every time we meet. But he brought me the first translations of his own work – into French, into English – almost casually, only later revealing that he had won an important poetry prize for them. Knowing a friend's poems is different from knowing that friend. Cevat's poems come from a world I know from talking to him, and yet, like all good poems, they are something new. They have their own authority, and their own life.

In Michael Hulse's translation what they have is a grown-up power of simplicity, at once lyrical and wry, rich and plain. They inhabit the large landscapes of Turkish life – steppes and forests, seas and mountains, in history and legend simultaneously. They inhabit also an extended world of modern politics. There are the moving poems written in Russia for Osip Mandelstam and Anna Akhmatova, poems which manage simultaneously to call up a legendary emotion – we *know* these events, we too have been moved by them, and yet the poet is making us feel them precisely again. There is the poem for Walter Benjamin, which begins with the poetry of myth and legend

Very late in life I learned
To lose my way in the forest

in which the writer of 'The Storyteller' moves in a kind of freedom

13

through a forest of city streets, having left his dreams behind in the "dark tangled maze of pages / In my childhood notebooks". Çapan's Benjamin is caught at the border, having undertaken a linear journey "under the guidance of history". His wry voice challenges the reader to "say if you like" that the last journey was a liberation. He repeats "say it / if you like". The connection between the traditional forest of tale-telling and the single journey compelled by historical events is riddling and unsettling. Mandelstam's words also are a "dark green forest". In 'A Thrush in an Acacia Tree' the poet remembers reading novels, and underlining sentences. One is "A train full of soldiers can change the course of history". Another is "A thrush began to sing in the acacia". The first is full of the unique linear movement of history; the second suggests some eternal recurrence or cycle starting its repetition. The sentences are part of the chattering stuff of the prose of novels. Abstracted, they become the bare, elegant bones of poetry.

Many of the poems in this collection concern exile and return, personal journeys that become archetypal pilgrimages. I particularly admire 'Epitaph', which is about Cevat Çapan's own father, who set out to sail to America and "somehow or other fetched up in Havana" – returning from there after bringing up a family, and stopping in Crete on the way to Turkey, where he met and married the poet's mother. There are only nine lines, the first four stating simply

> The islands. He was a man who loved
> The islands as much as women.
> A man from a village in the mountains
> Who made coffee for the city people.

The following spare six lines take the man from Turkey to prison in Algiers, from Marseille to Havana "in the reign of Abdulhamit II", adding history to geography. In 'From Erzincan and from Kemah (The sweethearts come dancing)' a voice remembers an uncle Nazim

> Whenever
> He drank he thought he was in Kars.

And the "years of exile. The deserts. And the Amazon". The memories mix New York, *Battleship Potemkin,* beautiful snows, and suddenly clearly

> Your mother was still a child.
> An immigrant from Crete:
> When she sang, she sang in Greek.

The speaker of this poem lives in dreams and stories, on his right the Sultan Melik, on his left the great Euphrates. He rides over the mountains on a dark stallion, and becomes Istanbul "my body shattered to pieces". The personal, the legendary, history and geography form another pattern. The same mingling of past and future, distant and written-about places, comes in 'The Wall' where the poet sits before three photos, one of "Cesar Vallejo, the Peruvian poet," who "died in Paris… coming down from distant mountains" and the other two of Akhmatova, one young, one old, "years after Kiev and / Petersburg", again mingling time and space, "Out of joint she seems. So close to the border". The border seems to be the border where Benjamin's journey failed or ended, and therefore Vallejo's Peruvian mountains remembered at death in Paris are and are not the same mountains, the same border.

When Cevat travels on the long journeys international poets travel on in these times, from Peru to Paris perhaps, from Istanbul to St Petersburg, he carries with him a case with the Turkish shadow puppets, made of painted camel-skin, whose images he projects on to white sheets and walls, the insubstantial dancing creatures of the professional storyteller's trade. Many of his poems are poems of storytelling, again both personal and traditional. His told stories run into dreams and personal histories. 'Compass' is the voice of the father telling his own story with the modern aid of an eternally youthful photograph

> You'd guess it wore me out but wouldn't
> See it in this photograph –
> My straw hat, linen suit, my silver-headed cane.
> When you were a child I told you tales
> Of Africa, the Amazon, Santiago and Havana:
> They were the whole of my youth, my manhood years.

This storyteller has returned to his original village to wait for the birth of the child to whom he will tell his stories.

A great deal – I sometimes think, too much – of modern poetry is about photographs. But the precise paring-down of Cevat Çapan's images to their essentials means that his poems about photographs contain whole worlds too. In 'Photography' the historical speed of the train full of soldiers returns, and the world is presented as a series of shots from a train window, a rag bag of shreds and tatters, a trapped outlaw "playing dice with his pitiless gaoler", a half-naked girl with her arm torn off, on a hoarding. This poem ends not with a grim warning but with the image of a singer poking fun, and

> It feels like a story that never grows old
> That age-old fire may grey with ash, but it glows and never dies.

And here the snapshot images have changed the linear train to the cycle of storied repetition. In 'Sepia' too, the storyteller stops the clock, and stills the leaves on the trees, mixing Turkish "Oguz the ghost" with "Mandrake and the Lone Ranger", feeding the imagination of his childish hearers in wartime with unfinished tales. In 'Bird's Eye View' the storyteller (the poet to his children?) tells of the migrating birds, inventing lions and alligators, naming imaginary islands. The listeners desire the migrations to the lake to be one-way, outward, they "didn't want to know" of the birds' return. And the poem – subtly, wisely – connects the silence when the birds flew off, of the growing older of the children – and the ending, not mentioned, but implied, of storytelling. In 'A Tale Half Listened To' the old storyteller is telling "of something that really happened" with "that same seductive glint of the Arabian nights" in his eyes, and in this case the listener does not need the end of the tale, which is about the last days of a painter, about a long march, travel and sickness, because the listener has already arrived in the shared silence at the end of the journey and the story.

In 'The Wellspring of Love' Çapan observes

> After a certain age, life is a chain
> Of infinite associations.

And this describes much of the experience of the modern world, and of modern poetry, as well as the experience of having lived long enough to acquire a bundle of memories and names and events. 'The Wellspring of Love' calls up in three lines Konstantin Nikolayevich Batyushkov, Pushkin's contemporary, who wrote elegies to Tasso "your very own Tasso" whose poetry liberated Jerusalem. Russia, a Russian poet, a great Russian poet whose ancestor was an African slave, Italian Tasso, Jerusalem, the Jerusalem of the crusaders, the Jerusalem of Israel, Islam and Christianity. In the next verse we have a putative "Swedish film" where a miner's lad is "trying to pronounce / the name Auguste Renoir correctly". A rustle of languages, a flicker of images. Another fine poem 'In Dreams begin Responsibilities' turns on the other kind of unexpected juxtapositions made in the unreal world of dreams. Douanier Rousseau is speaking like a Turkish sailor about a wind. "Madame Yildize" in a Cretan accent is telling a story about a shepherd on a black mountain, who saw a green tent where "the Green Lady is sitting, weeping, weeping". These clear colours are the stuff of Çapan's complex simplicity, and his landscapes have a Turkish version of Douanier Rousseau's paradisal strangeness and dream familiarity. That poem ends with a minstrel arising from the waters, as the dreamer comes down from the mountain, through the mist to the plain, and crosses to the island of Ahdamar on a raft with his father. The minstrel dries his saz, and sings, and "a voice" returns to the mountains and the plain from the water and the island. In 'The Wellspring of Love' the poet weaves Pushkin, Tasso, Swedish film and French painter, a woman singing "The Grieving Night" and the "shards of glass hearts" on the streets, into a new affirmation. Again there is the wry, humorous tone, which merges with complete ease into the lyrical. In the song

> The woman's troublesome lover kills off the cynic
> Within and far away in the Crete of my dreams,
> The pines reflected in the waves are burnished by the stars.

Çapan ends his poem with an address to poetry, who has "rendered the winds and storms so eminently useful". And states that his life has served to give beautiful names to his children

> Nigâr, Leylâ, Alişan.

It has also served to put a whole world together out of the endlessly renewed fragments and images.

A.S. Byatt 2001

from
RETURN, DOVE, RETURN
DÖN GÜVERCİN DÖN*'den*

KUŞLAR MIDIR ONLAR?

Buradan
Bu külrengi düzenden uzakta
Fenikeli martılar olmalı
Sevişen,
Sevişmeyi düşünmeden.

BOZKIR

Denizi özledik, denizi,
denizin alçalıp yükselişini
külrengi günlerde uçuşan
ak martıları,
büyük sessizlik içinde
geceye doğru
aydınlık, ılık
denizi özledik.

YAZIT

Adaları seven bir adam,
Adaları da kadınlar kadar.
Bir adam, gelip dağ köylerinden,
Han kahvelerinde duran.

Bir köylü, imparatorluğun payitahtında.
Bir kaçak, Cezayir zindanlarında.
Bir yolcu, Marsilya'dan.
İkinci Abdülhamit'in padişahlığında
Kalkıp Havana'ya giden babam.

ARE THEY BIRDS?

Far away,
far from this dreary grey scene,
surely there must be Phoenician seagulls
making love
not taking a moment's thought.

THE STEPPE

The sea, the sea,
how we have longed
for the sea, the rise
and fall of the waves,
the white gulls flying
on the grey dull days,
on in the vasty
silence to the night:
how we have missed
the bright, warm sea.

EPITAPH

The islands. He was a man who loved
the islands as much as women.
A man from a village in the mountains
who made the coffee for the city people.

A peasant, in the Empire's capital. Escaped
from prison in Algiers. Outward
bound from Marseille. My father. Who,
in the reign of Abdulhamit II,
somehow or other fetched up in Havana.

AÇIĞA DEMİRLİ BİR GEMİDEN

Dağın eteklerinde orman –
çam, sedir, ulu çınarlar...
Birbirini seyrediyor aynasında denizin.
Çamlar pürleriyle suskun,
sedirlerin gözleri uzakta,
"Ölünceye kadar seninim," diyor denize
kendi gölgesinde yanan bir çınar.

KIŞ BİTTİ

"Vedalaşmaların ilmini yaptım ben,"
Sürgünlerin uzmanlığını.
Bir vapur nasıl kalkar bir limandan.
Tren nasıl acı acı öter, öğrendim.

Yıllarca mektuplarla yaşadım.
Kaçak tütün, yasak yayın
Larla beslendim.
Unutmadım. Unutmadım.

En çok yelkenleri özledim
Bozkırın buzlu yalnızlığında.
Dağlar yoktu, dağlar yoktu,
Rüzgârlara yaslandım.

Çılgın mıydım, tutsak mıydım
Yüreğinde karanlığın?
Kan kurudu –
Ben gül oldum açıldım.

FROM A MOORED BOAT

The forest, on the mountainside –
pines and cedars, mighty planes,
watching each other in the mirror of the sea.
The needled pines are silent.
The gaze of the cedars never wavers.
A plane tree, burning in its own shade,
murmurs, "I am yours unto death."

WINTER IS OVER

"I've studied the art of farewell,"
specialized in exile.
I've learnt how a boat puts out from port.
Learnt the bitterness of a train whistle.

For years I lived on letters, lived
on smuggled tobacco, banned
publications. I've not forgotten a thing.
Nothing. Ever.

In the icy loneliness of the steppes
the sails at sea were what I missed the most.
There were no mountains, no mountains:
I leant back on the winds.

Was I out of my mind? A prisoner, say,
in the heart of darkness?
The blood dried –
and I was a rose, blown into flower.

ÖLÜMSÜZ

Sözcüklerinin
  koyu yeşil
    karanlık ormanına
     dalıyorum gene
      Osip Mandelştam.

Bilinmeyen
  mezarını arıyorum
    kulağımı
     toprağa dayayıp.

Yeraltının
  sessizliği içinde
    soluğuna biçim veren
     birer atardamar
      kımıldayan dudakların
       duyar gibi
        oluyorum.

Üzerinde
  kızılkara büyüyen
    bu buruk böğürtlenler
senin zengin yoksulluğun
  görkemli züğürtlüğün
    tek mirasın.

IMMORTAL

Again I'm entering
the dark green forest
of your words,
Osip Mandelstam.

I'm searching
for your nameless grave,
putting my ear
to the ground.

In the silence of the soil
I almost hear your lips
moving, like the blood
that shaped your breath.

Bittersweet blackberries
grow on the grave:
your rich poverty, splendid
bankruptcy, one and only testament.

UMUT

Nadejda. Voronej. Osip Mandelştam.
Yumuşak hecelerini ezberliyorum
bu adların.
Sanki hep gözümün önünde
şairi götürmeye gelen siviller,
birlikte geçirdiğiniz sürgün,
Osip'in kestiği elmas dizeler
Nadejda'nın belleğine gömülen.
Kar altında koğuşlar, kulübeler,
çalışma kampları, sanatoryum,
buzlu traversler. Sonra
nasıl yitirdiniz birbirinizi,
nerede çözüldü eller?

DÖNÜŞ

Yıllar sonra
odanın kapısını açınca
senin yerine
arkası dönük iki kadın görüyorum
yaşları belirsiz
biri kollarını balkonun korkuluğuna dayamış
öbürü kapının pervazına yaslanmış
uzanıp giden ovaya bakıyorlar
akşam serinliğinde.
Bakışlarının ucunda
mor dağlar yükseliyor
ve inen davarın
çan sesleri duyuluyor uzaktan.
Kapıyı aralık bırakıp
alacakaranlıkta
dağın doruğuna tırmanıyorum
yorgun atımın yedeğinde.

HOPE

Nadezhda. Voronezh. Osip Mandelstam.
I am learning the soft syllables
of these names by heart.
It is as if it were always before my eyes –
the secret police taking the poet away,
the exile you passed together,
the diamond lines incised by Osip
buried in Nadezhda's memory.
Snow-covered barracks, huts,
labour camps, the sanatorium,
the iced-up tracks. And then,
where did you lose each other,
when was the clasp of your hands loosed?

RETURN

Back. Years later. But
when I open the door
I see two women with their backs to me
where you would have stood.
Who can say how old they are?
One is resting her arms on the balcony rail.
The other's leaning in the doorway.
Both are gazing out across the plain,
the level distance stretching far
in the cool of dusk
to where, at the vanishing point,
the mountains are purple
and bells of flocks
on the homeward slopes
are a faraway sound.
Leaving the door ajar
in the fading light
I climb behind my weary horse
to the mountaintop.

BİR DELİ DÜLGER

Bak gene şaşırtıyorum seni
kış ortasında bir cemre
gibi düşerek kapının eşiğine
bir kuşluk vakti.
Cebimde yaz güneşi,
kırlangıç hızı,
gülkurusu,
ağustosböceği.

Ah, ne çok şarkılar öğrendim
gurbette,
kâğıt oyunları,
gözbağcılık,
acılı yemek tarifleri.
Balkonuna tırmanırken
geceye gizli,
aklıma takılan bu sarmaşık
sabahsefası mı,
hanımeli mi?

YAVAŞ ÇEKİM

Sonra akıl almaz resimleri çıktı
Gazetelerde,
Mektupları yayımlandı
Ölümünü yalanlayan.
Ve sanki o resimlerle,
Mektuplarla birlikte
Yepyeni bir hayata başladı
Aramızda
Geçmişe doğru.

A MAD CARPENTER

Surprise! Here I am again,
a midwinter sunstone
fallen one morning
on your threshold,
the summer sun
in my pocket, the swiftness
of the swallow,
this grubby shade of pink,
a cricket.

Ah, those songs
I learnt to sing
in exile, games
and tricks with cards,
the recipes for spicy dishes.
And when I climbed
to your balcony, under
cover of the night, that creeper
I couldn't get out of my mind –
was it honeysuckle
or morning-glory, hmm?

SLOW MOTION

Then one day
the papers were full
of those photographs,
those letters of his
that took the wind
out of death's sails.
And with the photos
and the letters
he seemed to be starting out
on a new life among us,
set toward the past.

WITTGENSTEIN

İçimin içime sığmaması
Canevimde çırpınan
Küçücük bir kuş
Olmasından mıdır aklın?

SENİNLE

Gün doğmadan,
Boğazın suları
Laciverdini daha yitirmeden,
Uzun bir sessizliğin
Ezgisini sindiriyorum içime,
Çayın rengi
Ve mavi dumanıyla
İlk cıgaranın.

Korkulu düşlerden uyanmışım
Delikanlı ömrümün
Sonu gelmez güzüne.

CEBREN VE HİLEYLE

Fena halde Londra'ya benzeyen
Kalabalık bir kentmiş
Cehennem.
Oysa küçük bir Venedik'ti
Krepen Pasajı
Tedavülden kaldırılmadan önce
Hileyle ve cebren.

WITTGENSTEIN

This irrepressible joy –
could it be the mind,
a little bird inside
beating its wings?

WITH YOU

Before the rising
of the sun, before
the Bosphorus waters
shed the darkness, I
take in the music
of a lengthy silence
with the colour of the tea
and the blue smoke
of the first cigarette.

Just now I woke
from the darkest dream,
back to the days of my youth,
back to endless autumn.

BRUTE FORCE AND CUNNING STEALTH

Hell may well have been
a city much like London.
But the Krepen Passage
was a little Venice
until they put an end to it
by cunning stealth
and brute force.

31

SINIRDA

Bak nasıl yağıyor içinin karanlığına
bembeyaz düşlerle ışıyan düşünceler
ve sen nasıl sarınıyorsun sessizce
bu azgın, bu azman kentin
kardan kefenine?

Bu senin sesin mi boğulurken duyulan,
bu uğultu, bu rüzgâr, bu fırtına
senin son soluğun mu?

Kar, uçsuz bucaksız kar
ve yeniden başlayan –

ON THE FRONTIER

See how it snows in your darkness,
snowing ideas radiant
with dreams all white,
and how you wrap yourself in silence
in the snow shroud
of this monstrous, hysterical city.

Is it your voice that one hears
while you are smothering?
This tumult, this wind, this storm,
is it your dying breath?

The snow, the vast and endless snow,
falls and goes on falling.

PUSULA

Nicedir uzaklardaydım:
uzak dağlar, uzak kıyılar, uzak --
dillerini bilmediğim yaban
insanlar arasında.

Uzayan bir uykunun karanlığından
düşlerin aydınığıyla vardım
yıllardır aradığım bu adaya.
Toprak, demir, şeker kamışı, ipek
ve elmasla uğraştım yıllarca.

Fotoğrafta gördüğün hasır şapka,
keten giysi, gümüş saplı baston
o yılların yorgunluğunu gizliyor
ustaca. Sana çocukluğunda anlattığım
Afrika, Amazon, Santiago, Havana
bütün gençliğimdi benim, olgunluğum.

Doğduğum dönülmez dağ köyüne döndüm
sonunda, geceleri sesiyle uyuduğum
derenin kıyısına.
Toprak dama, tandıra, boğma rakıya.

Beni tanıyasın diye bir gün
doğmanı bekledim sabırla.

COMPASS

Long time I was far away:
distant mountains, foreign shores.
I travelled among unknown men
with foreign languages and laws.

Then as if waking from the dark
of sleep, in a brightness of dreams,
I reached this island I'd been looking for
for years. And for years I worked:
iron, sugar cane, silk and diamonds.

You'd guess it wore me out, but wouldn't
see it in this photograph –
my straw hat, linen suit, my silver-headed cane.
When you were a child I told you tales
of Africa, the Amazon, of Santiago and Havana:
they were the whole of my youth, my manhood years.

And in the end I headed back
to the mountain village I was born in.
There I'd fall asleep by the stream,
listening to the flow, in a village
of clay-tiled roofs and earthen ovens and raki.

And patiently, so one day you would know me,
I waited till the time that you were born.

Nerede mi kalmıştık?
Elbette loş koynunda
çalgılı bir kahvenin,
zaman nasıl bir zaman
sonra kaç mevsim geçti.

Denizi ilk gördüğümde
ağzımda peksimet küfü,
tabakamda tömbeki.
Hey benim Nazim Dayım
Kars'a giden içerken.

Sonra o uzun sürgün
çöllerde, Amazon'da,
adımı da unuttum
"Şen Dul"u seyrederken,
gençliğim orda kaldı.

Dışarısı New York'tu
ne güzel kar yağıyordu,
İçerde "Potemkin"le
"Dünyayı Sarsan On Gün" –
Kars'a gidelim, yeğen!

Çok gezdim, az yaşadım
Zamanla yarışırken,
annen daha çocuktu
Girit'ten bir mübadil
Rumca şarkı söyleyen.

Düşlerim sılamdı benim,
sağımda Sultan Melik
solumdan Fırat akar
doru kısrak üstünde
Munzurları aşardım.

Sonra İstanbul oldum
her yanım darmadağın
bir gün Gülhane Parkı'ndaymışım
bir gün Burgaz'da dalgın
her yanım darmadağın.

FROM ERZINCAN AND FROM KEMAH
(THE SWEETHEARTS COME DANCING)

You ask me where we were? In
the sweetness and the dark, where else –
where music was playing.
O what a time it was,
how many seasons have passed.

When first I saw the sea
there was a taste of biscuit
in my mouth, tobacco in my pouch.
O my uncle Nazim, whenever
he drank he thought he was in Kars.

And then the years of exile.
The deserts. And the Amazon.
I even forgot my name
watching *The Merry Widow*.
I spent my whole youth there.

Outside, it was New York,
"beautifully snowing".
Inside, it was *Battleship Potemkin*,
Ten Days that Shook the World.
Let's go to Kars, nephew!

Too busy running my race with time,
too busy travelling to live.
Your mother was still a child.
An immigrant from Crete:
when she sang, she sang in Greek.

My dreams were home to me:
on my right stood Sultan Melik,
on my left the great Euphrates flowed.
On a dark stallion, over
the mountains of Munzur I rode.

And then I was Istanbul,
My body shattered into pieces.
One day I was in Gülhane Park,
the next on Burgaz Island, lost,
my body shattered to pieces.

from
NATURAL HISTORY
DOĞAL TARİH'*ten*

TAŞ BASKISI

El eleydiler,
yerdeki toz toprağın içinden
seyrediyorlardı gökteki bulutları
külrengi denizi.
Bir yerden vinçlerin gürültüsü
geliyordu, doldurulan, boşaltılan
şilepler,
mavnalara bindirilen vagonların
tekerlekleri arasından
bir çeşmeyi, bir ağacı, bir
kırlangıç yuvasını görüyorlardı sanki.

Öyle duruyorlardı.
Bildikleri bütün sözcükleri susarak
yineliyorlar, ezberlerindeki
renklerin birbirine akarak
biriktirdiği gölde
bir kayığın yosunlu bir iskeleye
yanaşmasını bekliyorlardı.
Belli belirsiz bir kaval sesi
karışıyordu sokak satıcılarının
bağrışmalarına.

El ele, bitkin, kaygılı bir ezinti içinde
han kahvesine bıraktıkları
tulum peyniri, bulgur, dut kurusu
avluda esans satan kitapçının
cam kutularından yansıyordu
kararan yüreklerine.

THE FIRE

Hand in hand they stood in the dust
  of the city, feeling the ashen breeze
  that came off the city waters, watching
  the clouds that passed them by
  in the alien sky.

The air was sheer and shrill
  with the clang of the docks, the loading noises
  of winches and cranes, the railway trucks
  that trundled onto the ferry.

And the two who watched
  saw the women who fetched the water in the village,
  the silver of the poplar leaves,
  the swallow's nest.
      There they stood,
  going over and over the rote
  of the words that spoke of home. There
  they stood, as if looking out for a boat
  that would moor at a mossy jetty
  where the lakewater patina
  shimmered like the world
  upon a retina.
     Amid
  the cries of the hawkers, like a bird,
  the single note of a flute. Faint. But heard.

Hand in hand they stood. How tired they were.
  They'd left the curd cheese and bulgur they'd bought,
  the bag of dried mulberries from the village,
  back in the pitiful two-by-four
  where their cousin made the coffee
  for the city people in the offices.

On sale beside the devotional books
  in the courtyard of the mosque
  were stoppered perfumes, unguents, cloying oils.
  The glass flaçons gave back distorted
  images. The heaviness of the heart.

Birden taş baskısı kitap
kapaklarının birinden
Hazreti Âli Düldül'üyle çıkıp geliyor
alıp Hayber Geçidinden Kan Kalesi'ne
götürüyordu onları Zülfikar'la
ikiye böldüğü gecede.
Gecenin bir dilimi soğuk çöl,
öbürü kızaran şafak, kızan kumdu.
El ele bekliyor, beklerken
kuru bir kan tortusuna dönüyordu
istekleri.

From the cover of one of the books
　　　Hazreti Ali rides his horse Düldül
　　　and spirits them away
　　　beyond the day,
　　　through Hayber, to the Castle of Blood,
　　　splitting the night with his sword.

The cold desert falls to one side of the blade,
　　　the blazing red of daybreak to the other.
　　　Hand in hand they stand
　　　waiting on the scorching sand,
　　　their longing and desire
　　　no more now than a streak of blood
　　　dried by the day's fire.

ÇOCUK YÜZÜN

Seni görünce,
bir sorun bir çözüm gibi
ipince ağdıydı içime.

O saat dönmeye başladıydı
dişlileri çarkların, tüten dumanla
göklere yükseldiydim birden
kendi türkümü dinlerken
o gürültüde.

Çiçekler, belli belirsiz başka renkleri,
başka kokuları kalabalıkların
dolduruverdiydi
bir memleketlimle paylaştığım
uzak odayı.

Sana bakıp
bütün sessizliklerini ezberleyince,
boğuk yankılarla bir sıla
bir gurbet gibi
yerleştiydi içme.

YOUR CHILDLIKE FACE

That moment I saw you
a question came to me
like an answer.

The cog notched home. The wheel began to turn.
Abruptly I was rising through the air
together with the smoke
that drifted upward from the chimneys,
my own song in my ears
in all that din.

The flowers, the different colours,
different smells of the crowd,
brimfilled the faraway room
I shared in those days with a countryman.

I looked at you, learnt all
your silences by heart,
and, deep within, my homecoming
and all its muffled echoes
settled like exile.

SUSIE PETSCHEK NERDESİN?

İlk kez 1955'te,
Floransa'da karşılaştığımız
Villa Fabricotti'de olamazın artık,
ne de motosikletle gittiğimiz
Fiesole'de.
Hatırlıyor musun Arno'yu, Eski Köprü'yü,
Santa Maria Novella'nın
serin servili avlusunu?
Tanıdığın ilk Türktüm ben,
sense ikinci kuşak bir Amerikalı,
yeniden Çekoslovakyalılaştıramayacağımız.
Dostluk böyledir işte:
yıllar sonra yediveren bir gül
belleğin çöllerinde.

WHERE ARE YOU, SUSIE PETSCHEK?

You can't go back. To Villa Fabricotti, say,
in Florence, where we met
in 1955. Fiesole,
where we rode up on a motorbike.
Remember the Arno? The Ponte Vecchio?
The courtyard of Santa Maria Novella,
the cypresses, the cool. I
was the first Turk you'd ever met, you
were a second-generation
all-American girl
who'd never be re-Czechoslovakized.
Such is friendship:
a rose in memory's desert,
flowering, unfading.

DUVAR

Karşımdaki duvarda üç resim:
biri Perulu şair Cesar Vallejo'nun,
bir güz Perşembesi Paris'te ölen,
inip uzak, çok uzak dağlardan.
Anna Ahmatova'nın öbür ikisi:
solda, bana bakan gençlik resminde
yıllar boyu dizelerine damıtacağı
acıyla beslenen gözyaşı ırmakları.
Sağdaki, yıllar sonra çekilmiş,
yıllar sonra Kiev'den, Petersburg'dan,
nice aşklar, acılar, suskunluklardan sonra,
Ağaran saçlarında, alnının kırışlarında
nice sonbaharlar nice ayrılıklar.
Ve hâlâ yakınlığın sınırına ulaşmanın
çılgınlığı.
Ve hâlâ gözlerinde o mavi yangın.

Three photographs on the wall
before me. One is of
Cesar Vallejo, the Peruvian poet,
who died in Paris one
autumn Thursday, coming down from distant mountains,
mountains so far away.
The other two are of Anna Akhmatova.
In the one on the left
she is still young, but I can see the suffering,
the tears that fell upon
her page. The one on the right was taken later,
years after Kiev and
Petersburg, after all of the loves and the griefs,
the pains and silences:
her greying hair and furrowed brow bear witness to
so many autumns and
so many separations. Out of joint, she seems.
So close to the border.
So close to closeness. So remotely close. And still
that blue fire in her eyes.

GÖÇ

Ayrılırken
turuncu pancurlarını
aralık bıraktığınız ev –
yıllarca
o açık pencereden girip çıkacak
çocukluk arkadaşın güvercinler
anılarının karanlık odalarına.
Arkanızdan bir kova suyla
sizi uğurlayan komşunuz
her akşam
tencereyi hızla maltıza vuracak
arka bahçede,
bir daha hiç karşılaşmayacağınızı
unutmak için,
sırtını denize çevirmiş,
gözleri dağlarda.

EMIGRATION

When you went away
you left the orange shutters
of the house
half open, so
in years to come
the doves, your childhood friends,
could enter and could leave
the dark rooms
of your memory
by that open window.
The neighbour who bade you farewell
by pouring water, wishing
you might flow as easy on your way,
puts a pot upon the fire
every evening
in the yard,
hasty in her ways,
wanting to forget
that she'll never see you again,
her back to the sea,
her eyes raised up to the mountains.

GİRİTTEN BİR MÜBADİL

Deniz kıyısındaki
o ahşap ev yıkılmadan,
taşlığında acı suyunu
kova kova çekip
taraçaya döken yorgun ihtiyar
Girit'ten getirdiği kitaplarını
kiloyla eskiciye satmadan,
teneke kutularda karanfil yetiştirir,
nargilesini fokurdatırdı denize karşı.
Deniz, yumuşak dalgalarla,
sallar, uyuturdu evi.
Evdeki öksüz kızlarını düşünürdü adam,
kim bilir kimlerle evlenip
nerelere gideceklerini.
Arada bir gemi geçip giderdi
uzaktan
uzaklara.

THE CRETAN EMIGRE

In times before
they pulled it down,
that wooden house
beside the sea,
before he sold
the books he brought from Crete,
by weight, to the man
who kept the junk shop,
the old man
who drew water
by the bucket
from the courtyard well
and splashed it on his terrace
used to grow carnations
in tin cans
and smoke his narghile
by the sea.
The waters gently
swayed the house,
rocking it to sleep.
And he would think
of his motherless daughters
in the house
and who they'd marry,
where they'd go.
And now and then
a ship would pass,
far out, bound
for distant shores.

ERZİNCAN ERZİNCAN

Cimin, Cencige, Hah –
köylerde dolaştık bütün gün,
Üzüm yedik bağlarda, buğulu,
bir başka dilde konuştuk.
Soluyan atlarımızla girdik geceye,
düşlere durduk.

DAĞLARDA MENEKŞELER

Bir keklik serinliğinde tırmanıyoruz
         dağa,
çam kokusu, kekik.
Köpüren deli çayın çağıltısı koyakta.
Uzakta, karşı yamaçta
yayılan davarın çan sesleri
ve gözlerinin göllerinde
boğulan kanlı başı güneşin,
Kulağımda sesin, yanık sesin:
"Haydut, beni nereye götürmektesin?"

54

ERZINCAN ERZINCAN

Cimin, Cencige, Hah –
all day we strolled
around the village,
in the vineyard
ate the grapes,
a misty bloom
fresh upon the skins.
We talked in another language.
And we entered the night
on our breathless horses,
ready for dreams.

VIOLETS ON THE MOUNTAIN

We are climbing the mountain
in a cool
of partridges, a scent
of pine and thyme,
the sound of the stream
foaming below. Far off,
over on the other slope,
the bells of the flock
are tinkling sheepishly,
and in the pools of your eyes
the blood-red sun is going under.
In my ears your voice,
your husky voice:
Wherever are you taking me,
you naughty man?

SAHNE AÇIKLAMALARI

I

Anası
sonsuz bir yumuşaklıkla bakıyor oğluna,
on altı yıl sonra bu ilk karşılaşmada –
bir başka kıtadan, bir başka dünyadan gelen
ve adresi bilinmeyen babasını andıran
bir yeniyetme.
Gene de boyu anasınınkini aşmış,
gözlerinin ışığıyla aydınlanıyor
ikamete zorunlu sürgünlere ayrılmış
bu yarı karanlık oda.

II

Bir başka ülkede, güze doğru,
bir başka sahne –
bahçeye açılan kapı, aydınlık oda;
solda, duvarda, Matisse'in
bir dergiden özenle kesilmiş
ve çerçevelenip asılmış
"Kırmızı Balıklar"ıyla "Yeşil Gözlü Kız"ı.
Sağda, masa başındaki orta yaşlı adam
dönmemeye karar veren oğluna
ne yazacağını düşünüyor
açık kapıdan odaya yalnızlığının yankısıyla
        dolan
denizin uğultusunu dinlerken.

STAGE DIRECTIONS

I

His mother looks at him
with infinite tenderness –
seeing him face to face
the first time now
in sixteen years,
this youngster from another
continent, another
world, so like his father
(whereabouts unknown).
He's taller than his mother, mind;
and this grim dusky room
the exiles at the camp have been assigned
brightens with the light that's shining in his eyes.

II

Another scene, another country,
summer fading to the fall,
a door swung open on the garden,
brightness in the room – and on the wall,
carefully clipped from a magazine,
'The Red Fish' and 'The Girl
with Green Eyes' by Matisse.
At a table to the right
a man in the mid years of his life
is wondering what on earth to write
to his son, who has decided
that he isn't coming back.
The soughing of the sea fills up the room
with aftermurmurs of his solitude.

III

Fırat boyunca yol alıyor tren,
suların akışına ters bir yönde,
yılların akışına ters.
Güllübağ istasyonunda bir yolcu
su dolduruyor
Sıvas'tan sonra yudum yudum
boşalttığı rakı şişesine.
Rüzgâra karşı yol alıyor tren,
geceye, gecenin soğuğuna karşı.
Murat'a karışmamış daha Karasu.
Suların kaynağına ulaşmayı
ummayan bir gidiş bu,
yolcunun varacağı dağ köyünün
uzağından geçen.
Gecenin içinde,
doğanın değil, tarihin karanlığında,
sabaha doğru, aydınlığa tutkun.

IV

Konakladığı han kale dibinde,
kale, dağın eteğinde, heybetli.
Han odasında
geceyi yıkayan ırmağın sesi.
Duvarlar ocaktan tüten
dumanla kararmış.
Sabah olsa, atına binse,
yarı yolda, gölgeli dere boyunda,
karşıcı çıkacaktır
yıllar önce askere giderken
beş yaşında bıraktığı yeğeni,
kekeleyerek konuşacaktır
elini öpmeye davrandığında.
Sonra, köye yaklaştıklarında,

III

Counter-current, contra-flow,
the train moves steadily along
the banks of the Euphrates,
against the waters, against the years.
At Güllübag station
the passenger who drained
his raki bottle slug by slug
along the line from Sivas fills it from a tap.
The train moves on, against
the wind, against the night,
against the cold of the night,
the confluence of Karasu
and Murat yet to come.
No prospect that the route will touch
that source where all the waters rise,
the mountain village where
the passenger is bound –
moving on through night, a darkness
born of history, not of nature,
on toward morning, like
a lover fascinated by the light.

IV

He puts up for the night
in the lee of a mighty fortress
on the shoulder of a mountain.
His room is awash with the rush
of the river laving the night.
The walls are black with the smoke
of numberless fires in the hearth.
He saddles up in the morning –
mid-journey, on that shady brookside track,
his nephew, who was only five
when he departed to the army,
will come to meet him, faltering
his halting words as he attempts
to kiss his hand; and then,

durp toprak damlara bakacaklardır
gün kavuşurken.

V

Bozkırda kara bir yılan gibi
    süzülüyor tren,
bozkırın o umursamaz boşluğunda.
Sonra dağlara sarılıyor,
başı dönüyor uçurumların
    kıyısında.
Gecede, gökten inmiş bir kuyrukluyıldız;
şafakta, bir çığlık.
Gün başlarken, soluyan yorgun bir aygır
    gibi
köy çocuklarını taşıyor
kasabaya, okula.

VI

Unutulmuş bir savaş alanı. Temmuz.
Sarısabır çiçekleri ateş içinde.
Tepeye yaslanan kalenin burçlarında
kartal yüklü bir rüzgâr.
Havuzlu lokantada birtakım yabancılar
    el işaretiyle
mermer yıkıntılar arasından
geçmişe açılan kapıların
yolunu soruyorlar.

VII

Acıklı bir ortaoyunu.
Palanga yarı audınlık.
Seyirciler arasından, kol kola,
sallanarak girerler Kavuklu'yla

60

as they approach the village,
they'll stop to watch the earthen rooftops.

V

Across the steppe
the train slides like a black snake,
across the indifferent emptiness
of the steppe. And begins the ascent
of the mountainsides, dizzy
at the edge of precipices.
At night, a comet from the sky.
At dawn, a scream.
As day resumes, a weary stallion,
it carries the village children
into town, to school.

VI

A godforsaken battleground. July.
The aloes are on fire.
Above the turrets of the castle
couched against the mountainside
a wind is blowing, fraught with eagles.
And at the restaurant by the fountain
tourists are signing a question:
where
are the gates that open
through the marble ruins
onto the past?

VII

This is the saddest comedy of all.
The stage half lit.
Enter Vladimir and Estragon
arm in arm

Pişekâr.
Zurnacı zurna olmuş horlamaktadır
dükkânla yeni dünya arasında.
Pişekâr, elinde pastav,
pişkin bir temenna çakar seyircilere,
yalnızlıktan yakınan gözlerle bakar.
Öbür elinde acıklı bir leylak.

GÜZEL YAZ

Bir şenlik oduydun sen
baktıkça ışıtan ve ısıtan,
ben küflü kitaplarda
sözcükler, anlamlar
ve tanımlarla boğuşurken,
bir şenlik odu ya da bir sağanak
sevdanın kızgın çeliğine
su veren.

El ele nasıl koşardık denize,
köpüklere, Temmuz'da?
Saçlarında ağustosböceklerinin sevinci,
kollarımda zincir sesi
zeytinlik yamaçlardan,
avlular, duvarlar, telörgüler
üstünden?

Bir şenlik odu – alevlerinde
isteğin kıvılcımları savrulurken
karanlık kış rüzgârlarını
denizin mağaralarına hapseden.

through the audience.
The piper is puddled,
peddling his piddly tunes centre-stage.
Vladimir bows to the crowd,
his bundle in one hand, in his eyes
the saddest melancholy, in
the other hand a sadder sprig of lilac.

THAT BEAUTIFUL SUMMER

You were a fire of joy,
your looks were light and warmth,
while there I sat
struggling with words and meanings,
the dictionary definitions,
you were a fire of joy,
a shower that tempered the hot
steel of love.

Remember how we'd run
to the sea, the surging foam, that July? –
in your hair the joy of crickets,
in my arms the sound of chains –
through the hillside olive groves,
the courtyards, the walls,
the barbed wire?

A fire of joy – sparks of desire
dancing on its flames,
while in the caverns of the sea
the dark winter wind abided.

BİR BAŞKA PENCEREDEN

O yanan yaz günleri,
kamaşmış koca bir cam göz deniz
ve hızla sararan bir karasevda:
Güz.

UZAK YAZ

Polatlı. Yazlık Sakarya sineması.
Anlaşılmaz bir şarkı söylüyor Zarah Leander.
Gündüzleri, elimde *Kâşifler Âlemi*,
şantiyede, çadırda:
belimde, küçük dayımdan kalma,
bir manevra kayışı.
Geceyle gün, yazla kış
ne zaman birbirine karışsa.
Ekvator'dan geçiyordur hep
Ümit Burnu'na varmadan.

ASKER

Uykusuz geceler bunlar
dağ başlarında, nöbette.
Uzakta, çok uzakta,
tek tük ışıklarını seçtiğin şehir
sokaklarında kısık sesle
şarkılar söylediğin.

FROM ANOTHER WINDOW

Those burning summer days,
the sea a vast
eye of glass,
dazzled and sad,
a rapid pallor: autumn.

CROSSING THE EQUATOR

Polatlı. The open-air Sakarya cinema.
Zarah Leander is singing some unintelligible song.
By day I'm reading *The World of Discoveries*
at the building site, in the tent, the site office,
round my waist a military belt
inherited from my young uncle.
Whenever night and day, summer
and winter blur in my mind,
I know Magellan's crossing the Equator.
Our ways invariably part
before I reach the Cape of Good Hope.

SOLDIER

Sleepless nights
keeping the watch
on the mountaintop.
Far off, the pallid
almost invisible
lights of the town
where you sang in the streets,
softly.

TREMOLO

Bir deniz kıyısındasındır şimdi,
geniş kenarlı hasır şapkanla
Ağzında külü uzamış bir cıgara
yem hazırlıyorsundur
deryadil balıklara.
Mintanın sevdanın rüzgârıyla
bir yelkenin talazlanışında.

TREMOLO

Yes, you must
be sitting
by the sea, wearing
your broad-brimmed
straw hat, on your lips
a cigarette
stacking ash,
preparing bait
for the great-hearted
fish of the sea,
your shirt
ruffling.

from
THE WELLSPRING OF LOVE
SEVDA YARATAN*'dan*

BEYAZ GECELERDE

Zaman gitgide daralıyor –
yola çıkmadan postalamak istiyorum
    sana bu kartı.
Lenigrad, biliyorsun, bir yazarlar kenti
Petersburg adıyla kurulduğu günlerden beri.
Neva'ya açılan kanallarında gezdirirlerken
Puşkin'in evini gösteriyorlar övünçle,
Dostoyevski'nin okuduğu mühendis mektebini.
Bir zamanlar Gogol'ün yürüdüğü köprülerin
altından geçiyoruz başlarımızı eğerek,
sonra kalabalığına karışıyoruz Nevski Caddesi'nin.
Her yerden altın kuleler görünüyor,
altın kubbeler, kışlık saray,
gezilmesi yıllarca sürecek müzeler.
Ve sağda, ağaçlı bir avlu içinde,
geçen yıl Anna Ahmatova'nin halka açılan evi.
"Anna Ahmatova, ünlü Rus ve Sovyet Şairi!"
Coğrafya baş döndürüyor Leningrad'da,
Tarih de öyle.

Time's running out on me:
before I leave I'll post this card to you.
Leningrad, as you know,
has always been a city of writers,
ever since it was built
as Petersburg. They take us on a tour
of the canals that give
upon the Neva, show us Pushkin's house;
they are Russian with pride.
And there is the engineering college
Dostoyevsky went to.
And these canal bridges we duck our heads
to pass under, Gogol
once walked across. Later we join the crowd
on Nevsky Prospect: no
matter where you stand you can see the domes,
the golden cupolas
and towers, the Winter Palace, museums
that would take years to see.
And, on our right, in a leafy courtyard,
Anna Akhmatova's
house, opened to the public just last year:
"Anna Akhmatova,
the famous Russian and Soviet poet!"
Geography makes you reel
in Leningrad, and so does history.

BİR ZAMANLAR AVRUPA'DA

John Berger'e

Dağların eteklerine akşam inerken
kapın çalınırsa, bil ki, bizizdir gelen.
İçerenköy'ün eski köşklerinden ney
ve tanbur sesleri yükselir ya
geçmişten geleceğe uzanan zamanda
çam kokulu yaz gecelerinde,
birbirinden ayrılmayan iki uyurgezer,
hâlâ o kayıp adreslerde dolaşan.

En son bir filmde gördük seni:
"Bana Bir Şey Çal".
İskoçya'da bir adada,
Mestre'de geçen bir öykü anlatıyordun
uçak bekleyen yolculara.
Otları biçme zamanı, diyorsun mektubunda,
kışın yazar, yazın ırgat!
Kitaplarında da biçilen otların,
bellenen toprağın kokusu: "Hınzır Toprak",
"Bir Zamanlar Europa'da",
şimdi de "Leylak ve bayrak".

Baharda,
dağların eteklerinden kar kalktığında,
kapın çalınırsa, beklenmedik bir anda,
bizizdir gelen:
          yedinci adam,
                    yedinci kadın –
leylaklar, bayraklarla.

ONCE IN EUROPA
for John Berger

When evening settles on the mountain slopes,
if you hear a knock at your door, it's us –
like the sounds of flute and lute
in the old summerhouses of İçerenköy
in a time that is past and present and to come,
in summer nights fresh with the scent of pine:
two sleepwalkers never to be parted,
wandering, calling at lost addresses.

Last time we saw you, you were in a film:
Play Me Something. On a Scottish island
you were telling a story set in Mestre
to passengers waiting for a plane.
It's time to make hay, you write –
a writer in winter and a labourer in summer!
They are rich with it too, your books,
with the scent of cut grass and tilled soil:
Pig Earth, *Once in Europa*,
and now *Lilac and Flag*.

In spring,
when the snow is gone from the mountain slopes,
if there's an unexpected knock at your door,
it's us –
          the seventh man,
                    the seventh woman,
with lilacs and flags.

ÇÖL

Ne zaman
    bir masa başına otursam
        sana bir şeyler yazmak için,
çocukluğumda seyrettiğim
    cambazlar geliyor aklıma,
elimdeki kalem
    birden
        o sırık terazi gibi uzuyor
ve ben
    çok geçmeden
        o usta cambazdan uzak
            acemi bir palyaço gibi
boşluğa yuvarlanıyor
    ve hoplamaya başlıyorum
        düşlerin yaylanan ağında.
Sonra,
    görünmeyen seyircilerimin
        kahkahaları çınlarken
            kulaklarımda,
kulaç atmaya çalışıyorum
    kurumuş bir gözyaşı denizinde.

DESERT

Whenever
    I sit down to write
        a line or two to you,
I remember the tightrope walkers
    I'd see as a child,
and the pen in my hand
    is suddenly
        the length of a balancing pole
and presently
    far from being
        a skilled jongleur
            I'm a fumbling clown
and fall into the void
    and bounce
        in the tensile net of dreams.
Then
    with the laughter
        still loud in my ears
            from the crowd I cannot see,
I try my flailing strokes
    in a sea of dry
        tears.

İZİNLİLER

Bir ağaç gölgesinde oturuyorlar,
yapraklarını dökmeyen bir ağacın gölgesinde –
konuşmadan, birbirlerine bakmadan.
Uzaktan
yokuşu tırmanan
bir kamyonun hırıltısı duyuluyor
öğle sıcağında.
Az sonra yola çıkacaklar:
geride kalacak yandaki ayazmanın serinliği.
Belki de hemşerilerinin sözünü ettiği
o hana varırlar gün kavuşurken.

Dağın eteğinde
onlardan habersiz
eskimeyen ay ışığı.

HOME LEAVE

They are sitting in the shade of a tree,
a tree that doesn't shed its leaves –
not talking, not looking at each other.
From afar
the throaty whine of a truck
is heard as it climbs the hill
in the noonday heat.
Soon they'll be off: leaving behind
the cool of the sacred spring by the chapel.
With luck they'll make the inn the villagers described
before the sun lays her cheek on the pillow of earth.

The moonlight on the mountainside
knows nothing of them
and is forever young.

Uzak bir yere taşınacakmış gibi
birer birer topluyorsun
dağınık bekâr odanda eski günleri.
Sandığın bir ucunda kadehinle leblebi,
telaşsız bir şarkının yankısı isli
    tavanda,
pencen yaz gecesine açık.
Her şey o açık pencereden doluyor
boşaltmaya elin varmayan
bu dört yıllık sığınağına:
sesler, kokular, meraklı çocuk yüzleri,
Gorki okuyan Lamise Öğretmen,
Candarmadan emekli Başefendi'yle
    Saatçi Hamdi.
Bu açık pencereden bakıyorsun
karanlıkta balığa çıkan kayıklarla
yalı mahallesinin tenha sokaklarına.
Kale arkasında düğün geceleri –
Çatalca'dan mı gelmiş çalgıcılar?
Davulcu kesin Kırklarelili!
Teneffüsle eşanlamlı okul bahçesi,
şafakla çay demleyen hademe Bekir.
Hatırlıyor musun, tarihten çok
coğrafyada coşardın: dağlar dağlar,
ırmaklarla bozbulanık denizlere akardın.

LEAVING THE JUNIOR SCHOOL

Packing up. Picking up,
one by one, the days gone by
in your untidy bachelor room,
as if you were moving somewhere far away.

In the chest
your raki glass
some roasted chick-peas.
On the ceiling
sooty black
the echo of a sweet and peaceful song.

Your window's open to the summer night.

It all crowds in
to this room that has been your refuge four years long,
this room you cannot bring yourself to strip:
voices, smells, enquiring children's faces,
Miss Lamise who loved Gorky,
the retired gendarme sergeant,
Hamdi the watch mender.

You're looking out of the open window
at boats pulling slow to the nightfishing waters,
deserted streets along the waterfront.
Wedding parties behind the fort –
are the musicians from Çatalca?
The drummer must be from Kırklareli!
The schoolyard meant the din of break.
Bekir the janitor brewed the tea at dawn.

Remember, teacher, how you would burn with the thrill
of geography far more than history:
mountains, mountains,
and with the rivers you'd flow
to the darkening waters of the sea.

"Demir, kömür ve şeker ve kırmızı bakır..."
Gene de, dördüncü sınıfta mı söz etmiştin
    Kerbela'dan?
Güle güle, delikanlı!
Bizi unutma, öğretmenim!

HANGİ SON MUTLU

Trenin penceresinden çekilmiş
bir resimden bakar gibi bakıyorsun dünyaya.
Dünya dersen, paçavralaşmış bir dünya:
ülkesinden kaçarken yakalanmış bir zorba
barbut atıyor çöl dekorlu
eski bir fabrika avlusunda gaddar gardiyanıyla.
Tahta perdede, afişteki yarı çıplak kızın
delikanlıya uzanan kolu yırtılmış.
Çalpara eşliğinde bir şarkıcı
dirlik düzenlik içinde bir dünyayla dalga
        geçiyor
karaparaların saçıldığı karanlık gazinoda.

İşin başlangıcı mı bu sonu mu, ortası mı?
Eskimeyen bir hikâye nerdeyse,
küllendikçe sönmeyen o eski ateş.

"Iron, coal and sugar and red copper..."
And was it in fourth year you told us about
the killing of Hussein at Kerbela?

Good-bye, young man!
Don't forget us, our teacher!

PHOTOGRAPHY

You're looking at the world as if
you were looking out of a photo shot
from the window of a passing train.

Tell me what you see.
A world in rags and tatters.
Tell me what you see.

An outlaw caught fleeing the country
playing dice with his pitiless gaoler
in the yard of a derelict factory.

Tell me what you see. A hoarding,
a girl on a poster, half-naked, reaching
out to a man, her arm torn off.

The pleasure gardens where illicit money goes
are in darkness now. The singer clicking his castanets
pokes fun at all things prim and proper, creatures great and small.

Is this the beginning? The middle? The end?
It feels like a story that never grows old.
That age-old fire may grey with ash, but it glows and never dies.

DÜŞLERDE BAŞLARMIŞ SORUMLULUKLAR

I

Serin bir su gibi esiyor üstümüzden rüzgâr.
"Poyraz!" diyor Gümrükçü Rousseau kırk yıllık
    bir denizci edasıyla
Üstad acaba Türkçe'yi kimden öğrenmiş?
Derken kırmızı bayraklı teknesi bacasını
    kırarak
nehirdeki bir köprünün altından geçiyor
poyraza aldırmadan.

II

Bir gece gezmesine gitmişiz komşularla;
Yıldıze Hanım bir masal anlatıyor Giritli
    ağzıyla kahvelerden sonra:
"Ey çoban çoban!"
"Söyle ağam!"
"Nerden gelirsin?"
"Kara dağdan."
"Kara dağda ne gördün?"
"Yeşil çadır kurulmuş.
İçine yeşil hanım oturmuş.
Ağlıyor, ağlıyor."

III

Bir ormanda kaybolmuşuz,
sen sımsıkı elimden tutuyorsun.
Birden yıldızların aydınlattığı
bir düzlüğe çıkıyoruz.
Uzakta,
            denizin sesi
ve katran kokusu
sabahı arayan
meltemin getirdiği.

IN DREAMS BEGIN RESPONSIBILITIES

I

The wind blows over us like fresh water.
"Le poyraz!" observes Le Douanier Rousseau,
with the air of a sailor who's been going to sea these forty years.
Whoever, I wonder, taught the Master Turkish, do you suppose?
Then his boat with its red flag
lowers its smokestack to pass below the bridge
not caring at all for the wind.

II

It seems in my dream that we pay an evening call
on the neighbours. After coffee, Madame Yildize
is telling a story in her Cretan accent.
"O shepherd, shepherd."
"What is it, master?"
"Where have you been?"
"On the black mountain."
"What did you see on the black mountain?"
"They've put up the green tent. Inside
the Green Lady is sitting, weeping, weeping."

III

It seems we are lost in a forest.
You are holding my hand tight.
Suddenly we come out
into a starlit clearing.
Far away,
                    the sound of the sea
and the smell of the bitumen
carried on the breeze
in quest of morning.

IV

Sislerin içinde
ağır ağır ovaya iniyoruz dağdan.
Burası Van, diyor babam.
Bir salla Ahdamar'a geçiyoruz.
Sonra bir âşık çıkıyor sulardan,
sazını kurutuyor okşayan elleriyle
ve uzaktaki ovayı kaplayan
bir ses yükseliyor
indiğimiz dağlara.

WALTER BENJAMIN
(1892-1940)

Hayatta çok geç öğrendim
yolumu kaybetmeyi ormanda;
by yüzden, büyülenmiş gibi aşkla,
    dolaştım durdum
sevdiğim şehirlerin sokaklarında.

Düşlerim
karanlık dehlizlerinde kaldı,
çocukluk defterlerimin yapraklarında.

Nelerden, nerelerden geçtim
kaybolan zamanın ardında.
Kaçmadım, kovalandım; kıstırıldım
    bir sınırda.

Belki de bir kurtuluştu
çıktığım son yolculuk
Tarih'in kılavuzluğunda.

IV

Slowly we're coming down from the mountain,
through the mist, to the plain.
This is Van, says my father.
We cross to the island of Ahdamar on a raft.
Then a minstrel emerges from the water,
dries his saz with a touch of loving care,
and a voice is uplifted, carrying over the plain
and on to the mountains from which we have descended.

WALTER BENJAMIN
(1892-1940)

Very late in life I learned
to lose my way in the forest.

I went on walking, like a man
stunned stupid with love,

along the streets of the cities I loved.
My dreams I left behind

in the dark tangled maze of pages
in my childhood notebooks.

Just passing through. So many, many places.
The long pursuit of times lost. No,

I did not run away, did not escape:
they caught me at the border.

Say if you like that my final journey
under the guidance of History

was a liberation: say it
if you like.

HAİKU GİBİ

I

Beş yıl sustuktan sonra
bu sözleri hangi seslerle fırlatmalı
geceye
havai fişeklerin sevinciyle?

II

Gecenin ağaran ucundan koparıyorum
sabahın
ilk kızılcığını.

III

Narı ikiye bölünce
kanlı gözyaşları dökülüyor
içinden.

IV

Narı da böl ikiye
korkma
artık ağlamayacak.

V

Sana ne söylemek isteyebilirim
gözlerinden
uzaklara bakarken

DO NOT BE AFRAID

I

Five years without a word. Tell me,
how shall we shoot the things we want to say
sky-high with the joy of fireworks
in the night?

II

I pick from the paling
approach of day the dawn's
first cornelian cherry.

III

Cut the pomegranate in two
and tears of blood
weep from the wound.

IV

Cut it in two. Go on.
Do not be afraid. The pomegranate
will weep no more.

V

Whatever could I want to say to you,
looking through your eyes
to faraway places.

VI

Yağmurdan bata çıka çamurlara
varıyorum pırıl pırıl
gözlerinin gölüne.

VII

İyi ki sapmışım
doğru evime giderken
sana yönelen yola.

VIII

Kırlangıçların saati –
demek taşradayız,
unutulmuş bir yaz akşamı.

IX

Altıma serdiğin geceyi
yıldızlarınla donatıp
üstüme örtmeyi unutma.

X

Usulca giriyorsun rüyalarıma,
çıt çıkarmadan
ve uyandırmadan halayıklarını.

VI

Raining. Walking ankle-deep
in mud. The glinting lakes,
your eyes. Home and wet.

VII

I did well to turn off
to your place on my way
straight home.

VIII

The hour the swallows love.
Here we are in the country
a summer evening in Oblivion.

IX

Remember, mantle me
in night, spread it under me,
deck it with your stars.

X

Gently you enter my dreams,
silent as the very air,
letting the sleeping slave girls lie.

KAYIŞ KASNAK VOLAN

Yakar bağır açık oturuyorum arka bahçede.
Yıllardır açmamıştım yakamı bağrımı.
Sanki bu bahçeyi de çoktan unutmuşum,
şurada teneke saksılarda fesleğen olduğunu;
bir zamanlar,
çocukların oynadığını tahta çitin ardında.
Bir ölüm sessizliği ölümlerden sonra.
Kuşlar da konarmış komşunun kurumuş ağacına.
Nerdeyse denizi göreceğime inanacağım
başımı kaldırsam.
Kötü günlerin iyimserliği bu.
Kaç kişi kaldı bu mahallede eski havuzlu
kahveden
gece vardiyasında birlikte
"Açmam açamam"ı söyleyen?

THE BELT, THE FRAME, THE FLYWHEEL

I'm sitting in the garden with my collar open.
Years it's been since I undid my collar.
I'd completely forgotten the garden, it seems,
the basil in those tin cans over there;
at one time,
children used to play behind the fence.
A mortal silence after so many deaths.
Birds are perched in the neighbours' withered tree.
I could almost believe that if I raised my head
I could see the sea. The hope of hopeless days.
How many of them are still alive
whom I used to know in the old café
by the pond, who used to sing
on night shifts: Wound, oh secret wound?

SEVDA YARATAN

Bu şehrin adları durmadan değiştirilen
    sokaklarında dolaşırken,
eski bir şarkıyı çağrıştırır bazen
    aklına takılır olmadık adlar.
Örneğin, Konstantin Nikoleyeviç Batyuşkov,
    Puşkin'in bir çağdaşı –
hani şu ölen Tasso'ya ağıtlar yazan –
    evet, senin Tasso'na,
Kutsal Kudüs'ü özgürlüğe kavuşturan.

Bir yaştan sonra, sınırsız bir çağrışımlar
    zinciridir hayat;
başka kokular, başka görüntülerle
    saldırır üstüne tekleyen belleğinle
ve birden başka adlarla uyanırsın
    bir dağ yamacında daldığın düşten.
Bir İsveç filminde miydi
    o küçük madenci çocuğu
Auguste Renoir'ın adını hecelemeye çalışan?

Her şey ne kadar külrengi ve dağınık
    gökle denizin maviliği ötesinde.
Bir kadın "Gecenin matemini" söylüyor öğle üzeri
    ve herkesten bir şeyler kalan bu sokaklarda,
kırılan camdan kalplerin parçalarını toplarken,
    belalısı gizlice zehirliyor içindeki aylak köpeği.
Ve uzakta, düşlediğim Girit'te, belki de,
    denize eğilen çamları yıkıyor yıldızlar.

Sonunda sana sığınıyorum, ey şiir,
    rüzgârları, fırtınaları yararlı kılan.
Yaşarken, güzel adlar koydum çocuklarıma:
    Nigâr, Leylâ, Alişan.

At times when you walk this city
    where the street names are forever changing
the curious names put you in mind
    of a song from days long gone – say,
Konstantin Nikolayevich Batyushkov,
    Pushkin's contemporary,
the one who wrote elegies to Tasso,
    your very own Tasso,
whose poetry liberated Jerusalem.

After a certain age, life is a chain
    of infinite associations;
into your flagging memory it bursts
    with other odours, other images,
and suddenly you waken from your dream
    on a hillside, other names in mind.
Was it in a Swedish film we saw
    the miner's lad trying to pronounce
the name Auguste Renoir correctly?

How grey it all is. And shattered. Beyond
    the blue sea and the sky. Noon,
and a woman is singing 'The Grieving Night'.
    Something remains of each of us on the street
where you can pick up the shards of glass hearts.
    The woman's troublesome lover kills off the cynic
within, and far away, in the Crete of my dreams,
    the pines reflected in the waves are burnished by the stars.

And so in the end I seek my refuge in you, poetry,
    who render the winds and storms so eminently useful.
My life has served to give beautiful names to my children:
    Nigâr, Leylâ, Alişan.

ESKİ YAZ

Eski bahçede, paslı sapını tutarken tulumbanın
küllenen ateşe sürdüğün cezve,
tozlu yaprakların gölgesinde çürüyen iskemlede
– bir yandan seni seyrediyorum –
gençliğin canlanıyor belli belirsiz:
Birlikte türküler söylerdik kısık bir sesle.
Gerçekten öyle güzel miydi dokunduğumuz her şey?
Bize mi öyle gelirdi soluduğumuz gece
bir baharatçı dükkanının bin bir çeşidiyle?
İster izinle dönelim gurbetten
tahta bavullarımızda Malatyalı Fahri'nin plakları,
ister sıla bildiğimiz dağ köyü,
toprak damında loğuyla, çırasıyla
ve gökyüzü yıldızlarıyla donatsın yaz gecelerimizi,
kekik kokusu bağışlayan bir yel eserdi
ve bilirdik, dağların ardındaydı her şey.
Çerkez eyerini ne zaman vursak kara kısrağa,
işte biz hep o dağları aşmak isterdik.
Sonra ne oldu bize? Nereye savruldu herkes?
Ve ben şimdi seni seyrederken
canlanan gençliğinle eski bahçede,
eprimiş çerkez eyeri, külrengi iskemle,
belli belirsiz bir türkü kısık bir sesle
yansırken tozlu yaprakları sılanın
acı sularında unutulmuş kuyunun

THAT SUMMER

We're in the old garden. You're
holding the rusty handle of the pump
and pushing the coffee pot back in the smouldering
charcoal of the fire. And I
am watching you, from the clapped-out chair
under the dusty leaves. I'm watching. And
your youth comes into focus, slow but sure.
Those songs we used to sing, in husky voices:
was everything we touched so beautiful,
or did it only seem that way to us?
Nights that were a store of spices,
a thousand and one rich fragrances in one.
Remember the time we were on leave?
Remember those records by Malatyalı Fahri
in our cases? The mountain village
that was home. Stone rollers on the clay-tiled roofs.
The pitch-pine kindling. Stars that lit
our summer nights. The wafting breezes
gifting us a scent of thyme –
and through it all, our certainty
that everything was out there, out beyond the mountains.
We'd mount the black stallion, vault
into its Circassian saddle, eager
to ride away. What happened to us, say?
Where is everyone now? And what has become of me,
as I watch you now, here in the garden
that takes us back to the old Circassian saddle,
an ash-coloured chair, or a melody
sung in a husky voice. What of
the dusty leaves of home,
reflected in the bitter waters
of the forgotten well?

DEĞİŞMEYEN

Her zaman o alaycı çağrı
denize koşarken bile:
"Beni seven arkamdan gelir!"
Ve sonra geriye dönmeden
kucaklaşmak sularla,
serinliğiyle köpüklerin
ve kulaç kulaç açılmak
sonsuzluğuna sevginin.

Her yaşta bir başka düşle
ve sarhoş bir gemiyle hep
sürdürdün bu yolculuğu
Kanaryalar'ına, Bermudalar'ına
bilmediğin denizlerin.
Gerçeğin ormanlarına dalsan da,
dinlensen de gölgesinde söğütlerin,
rüzgârdı, yelkendi hep özlediğin.

Saç damdan günün ilk ışığı
ne zaman süzülse koğuşa,
şafağın meltemiyle
otlar türküye dursa,
kişnerdi anlamsız talimlerle
evcilleşmiş sandığın
düşteki o kösnül atlar
ve başlardı içindeki fırtına.

IMMUTABLE

Always that ironic invitation,
even running to the sea:
"If you love me, follow me!"
Then without turning back
to embrace the waves
and the cool of the foam,
and to swim stroke by stroke
to a love without end.

At every age, with a different dream
but on the selfsame drunken boat,
you pursued this voyage
to the Canaries, to the Bermudas,
on seas unknown to you.
Times you strayed in forests of the real,
times you rested in the shade of willows –
but what you always looked for was the wind and the sails.

Whenever the first rays of daylight
filtered through the tin roof
into the barracks
and the grass started to sing
with the breeze of the dawn
the horses of lust, which you thought tamed
by witless dressage, stampeded –
and the tempest within you raged afresh.

YAZ KAPILARINDA

Her şey bir güzel kız için yazılır, diyor.
Kırkına yakın, yılgın biraz.
İsteksizce yanıtlıyor derginin sorularını.
Öğrenci derneğinde konuştuğu akşam
uzaklarda gibi dinleyenlerden, güvenle konuşuyor –
üst üste kazandığı yenilgilerin güvenliği içinde.
Oyunlarından sahneler geçiyor gözlerimin önünden,
değişik zamanlarda, değişik sahnelerde izlediğim:
çürüyen bir şey, çocukluktan erginliğe geçerken,
yarı kaçık soylular, saray artıkları, kırgın bilgeler,
şehvetle kutsallığın kucaklaştığı tenha köşeler…
Sonra kurtulmak için boğuntusundan günlük kokulu
        karanlıkların,
kırlar, kırlar ve uçsuz bucaksız ovalar.
"Bir ırmağın kıyısında sevişmiştik o yaz."
Her şeyi bir güzel kız için yazmış olmanın erinciyle
        açıyor yaz kapılarını
yenilgilerinin güvenliği içinde.
Yorgun, ama hâlâ içinde o yakıp tüketen özlemi
        bilinmeyenin.

THE WRITER

He's never written a word (he says)
that wasn't written for a beautiful girl.
Now he's nearly forty. Tedium
vitae's stealing up. The answers he gives
to interviewers from magazines
are weary. Talking to a student group
one evening, he seems far away
from his audience, though he speaks with confidence,
a confidence born of recent failures.
Scenes from his plays appear before my eyes,
scenes I saw at different times,
on different stages: misadventures on the road
from childhood into adulthood,
half-mad aristos, toadies at court,
wise old men taking umbrage,
hideaways where lust and holiness
go hand in glove. And then:
to get out of the incense fug and dark,
to fields, green country, boundless plains.
"We made love on a riverbank that summer."
He opens his summer gates
with all the serenity of mind
that comes of writing for a beautiful girl,
with all the confidence of his failures.
Tired he is. But in him still
the fire to discover burns.

SEPYA

Sonra sonundan başlardı hikâyesine,
o mutlu ya da acıklı sonu açıklar,
asıl iş anlatılanda değil, anlatanda, derdi.
Biz de bakakalırdık onun sesinin büyüsüne
      kapılıp.
Kimdi, nereden gelmişti, neden öyle parlıyordu
      gözleri?
O söze başlayınca, saatler durur,
yapraklar titremezdi ağaçlarda.
Bir yolculuğa çıkarırdı bizi peşine takıp;
gece gündüz, dere tepe
belli belirsiz zaman birimleri, yer adları –
karartma geceleri, üç aylar, sevdalı bulut,
köşede yanık kokulu tahmis,
karpuzlarını mumlarla aydınlatan manav,
Cibali'den Küçükmustafapaşa'ya götüren
      arnavut kaldırımı sokaklar,
tek kollu Gazi Eniştem, fırında,
ekmek karnelerini kareli bir kağıda yapıştıran.
Sonra Hayalet Oğuz belirirdi
Mandrake ve Maskeli Süvari'yle kol kola,
cebinde açık saçık resimler.
Ve Ali Nizami Bey, Eyüp-Keresteciler otobüsünden
      iner
Tarzınevin'le Kuzguncuk'a geçerdi.

Mevsim yaz, aylardan Temmuz'du,
sonu mutlu mu, acıklı mı,
belli olmayan bir masal.

Then he'd tell his story, starting
at the end, beginning by giving
the sad or happy ending away, explaining
the secret's in the teller, not the tale.
And we'd drop everything and gape,
entranced by the spell of his voice.
Who was he? Where was he from? What
made his eyes shine with that light?
He spoke and the hands stopped on the clock.
He spoke and the leaves kept still on the trees.
He'd take us on a journey and
we'd follow him, all day, all night,
up hill, down dale, oblivious of time and place –
nights of black-out, the three sacred months,
the cloud in love, the smell of coffee
roasting round the corner, the greengrocer
displaying his watermelons by candlelight,
the cobbled streets that lead from Cibali
to Küçükmustafapaşa, and
my one-armed veteran uncle at the bakery
sticking the ration coupons on a long sheet of paper. Then
Oguz the Ghost would appear, arm
in arm with Mandrake and the Lone Ranger,
dirty photos in his pocket.
Ali Nizami Bey got down from
the Eyüp-Keresteciler bus and crossed
to Kuzguncuk on the Tarzınevin.

It was summer, then. July.
A story with a sad or happy ending
never to be told.

KUŞ BAKIŞI

O göçebe kuşları da merak ederdin sen,
yılın hangi ayında geldiklerini,
gelirken hangi enlemlerden geçtiklerini,
yuvalarını nerelerde yaptıklarını...
Turuncu, altın sarısı, siyah tüylü o kuşlar.
Onları anlatırdım sana kış geceleri,
aştıkları lacivert denizleri,
adlarını uydurduğum kimsesiz adaları.
Arslanlar kükretirdim geride kalan ormanlarda,
filler dolaştırır, timsahlar dövüştürürdüm
çamurlu ırmaklarda.
Derken kızıl kiremitleri görünürdü bir kıyı
köyünün dağınık damlarında.
Ve bahar yağmurları yağdıran bulutların
arasından süzülür bir gölün kıyısına konarlardı
kuşlar.

Dönüşlerini anlatmamı istemezdin hiç.
Hep kalsınlar, derdin, o gölün kıyısında
ya da yuvalarını yaptıkları saçak altarında.
Kışa doğru, geceler uzar, koyulaşırdı karanlık.
Sen büyürdün, büyürdü göçebe kuşların
giderken aramıza bıraktıkları sessizlik.

BIRD'S EYE VIEW

They fascinated you as well, the migrating birds,
which month of the year they arrived, which parallels
they crossed as they flew on, and where
they built their nests... those birds
with orange and golden plumage and black.
I used to tell their tales on winter nights,
tell you of the dark blue seas they crossed,
the desert islands – I made up the names.
I made the lions roar in forests
as the birds flew on their way, the elephants
stomp about, the alligators fight in muddy rivers.
Below the birds appeared the red-tiled roofs
of coastal villages. And gently on their way
the birds flew on, through rainclouds, till
they touched land on the margin of a lake.

You didn't want to know of their return.
You wished they'd stay forever by the lake,
or under the eaves where they'd built their nests.
As winter came, the nights grew longer, darkness darker,
you grew older, and the silence left behind with us
when the birds flew off
grew deeper, deeper.

SONU

Buğulu camda bir kar masalı
giderken ince parmaklarınla yazdığın:
"Dağın dibindeki ininde…"
Okumaya çalışıyorum
süzülüp akan alttaki satırları.
Anlaşılmıyor kimlerin murada erdiği.
Çıkıp büzülüyorum ben de o bildik
        kerevete;
hohlayıp ısıtmayı deniyorum
        parmaklarımı
yarı uyanık gördüğüm düşte.

THE END

Before you left
you traced a snowtale
on the misted
window pane
with a slender finger:
"In the cave
below the mountain…"

I'm trying to read it
as the lines
dissolve and run,
unable to make out
whose happy end it was
the story told of.

And I snuggle for warmth
on the sofa I love
and curl into a knot,
breathing on my clenched
fingers for the warmth.
All of this a waking dream.

NEW POEMS
YENİ ŞİİRLER

SİMYA

Yan yana gelince sözcükler,
kendi anlamlarından soyunup
bir yağmur tanesi gibi
yuvarlanıveriyorlar
kavruk otlarına sessizliğin,
ya da parlıyorlar
bir gözyaşı gibi
gencecik ayın
inceliğini yansıtan.

Uzaktan,
kanlı naraları duyuluyor
dev tutkulu cücelerin
yan yana gelen
sözcüklerin arasından.

ALCHEMY

When words get together
and lie side by side
they take off their clothes
and roll in to the silence
of dried-out grass
like raindrops, or
they shine like tears
that replicate
the tender crescent of the moon.

But from far away
amid the words
that lie there side by side
are heard the vast and bloody roars
of dwarfs forever craving *more*!

YARISINI DİNLEDİĞİM BIR MASAL

Haydi bir sayfa daha çevirelim denizden,
üzerinde beyaz yeleli aslanların dolaştığı bir sayfa –
Bu kez gerçek bir olayı anlatıyor eski masalcı,
gözlerinde gene binbirgecenin ayartıcılığı,
sesinde uzaklıklar, deli rüzgârlar,
körkuyular, yolculuklar, kervansaraylar.
Çiçekler çizen, onları renk renk boyayan
bir ressamın son günleri anlattığı.
Birbirine karışıyor sözlerle görüntüler:
O uzun yürüyüş, okunaksız bir yazıyla yazılmış
mektupları andıran kalabalıklar,
hastaların yüzlerindeki acı.
Her yolcu gibi, nereye gitse,
sılasını yüreğinde taşıyan bir yolcu.
Masalcı arada türkü söyler gibi mırıldanıyor,
sonra bize sevgiyi sezdiren
bütün o sevdiklerimizin sesiyle
yeniden başlıyor anlatmaya.
Ama artık ben orada değilim,
ya da şimdiden
yağmurunu dökmüş bir bulut hafifliğinde,
karanlığın sessizliği,
sessizliğin bize düşen mutluluğu içinde,
masalcının masalının sonunda
varacağı yerdeyim.

Let's turn another page of the sea,
a page on which the white-maned lions roam.
This time the old story-teller is talking
of something that really happened. But in his eyes
that same seductive glint of Arabian Nights,
in his voice the distances, wild winds,
dry wells, voyages, caravanserais.
The tale's about the last days of a painter
who draws flowers and paints them different colours.
His words and the images coalesce;
the long march, the crowds
for all the world like an illegible letter,
the pain on the faces of the sick.
Like every other traveller, bearing
the ache of longing in his heart on every journey.
The story-teller talks in a soft croon
as if he would break into song; then in the voice
of those who bring love before us, resumes the tale.

But I am no longer there. I'm already
where the teller's journey has its destination,
but having arrived I'm as light as a cloud
that has shed its burden of rain,
and within the silence of darkness and our share
                              of the bliss of silence
where the story-teller's destined to arrive.

BİR ARDIÇKUŞU AKASYA AĞACINDA

O yaz,
bol bol roman okudum,
denize girdim kimsesiz kumsallarda;
rüzgârların, balıkların adlarını öğrendim.
Nice cümlelerin altlarını çizdim
kırmızı kalemimle.
Örneğin,
"Asker dolu bir tren tarihi değiştirebilir."
Sonra gene aynı kitaptan,
"Bir ardıçkuşu şakımaya başladı akasya ağacında."
Geceleri,
sararan otların üzerine uzanıp
bir açıkhava sineması seyrettim
gökteki yıldızlardan
ve altını çizdiğim cümlelerle konuşturdum onları,
uzaktan bir çağlayanın sesi karışıyordu
yıldızların mırıltılarına.
Gene de duyabiliyordum Adil Nuşiran'ın huzurunda
hayat denilen bu acılar denizinde
en acımasız dalganın ne olduğu konusunu tartışan
üç bilge kişiyi.
Odama çekilip yatmadan önce,
tarihi değiştirebilecek asker dolu o trenin
hızla geçtiğini duydum,
sonra da
akasya ağacında şakımaya başlayan ardıçkuşunu.

Karşıda Midilli,
denizin ötesinde, sessiz.
Bu sessizlik sanki
o sevdalı kadını
bin kulaklı geceye fırlattığı çığlık
binlerce yıl önce.

A THRUSH IN AN ACACIA TREE

That summer
I read novels, novels, novels,
swam on deserted beaches, learnt
the names of winds and fish.
I underlined any number of sentences
in red pencil.
                    Such as:
"A train full of soldiers can change the course of history."
Another from the same book:
"A thrush began to sing in the acacia."
At night I lay on my back in drying grass
watching the stars in the sky, as if
I were in an open-air cinema: in
my imagination they held conversations
using the statements I had underlined.
Far away, the sound of a waterfall
mingled with the sotto voce of the stars.
Yet still I heard the three sages debating
which was the most inexorable wave
in the ocean of suffering we call Life.
They were discussing the question in Adil Nushiran's yard.
Before I turned in for the night, I heard
the train full of soldiers that could change the course
of history pass at high speed, and then
the thrush begin to sing in the acacia.

Mytilene lay across the sea, in silence,
a silence like the scream
of that amorous, passionate woman
cast upon the night of a thousand ears.

CEVAT ÇAPAN was born in Darıca near Istanbul in 1933. He studied at Robert College from 1945 to 1953, read English at Peterhouse, Cambridge from 1953 to 1956, taught English Literature and Drama in the English Department of Istanbul University from 1960 to 1980, and worked as Professor of Drama in Mimar Sinan University from 1980 to 1996. He is currently Professor of English at the Yeditepe University in Istanbul.

His first book of poems *Dön Güvercin Dön* (*Return, Dove, Return*) was awarded the Behçet Necatigil Prize in 1986. His later poems were collected in two other volumes *Doğal Tarih* (1989) and *Sevda Yaratan* (1994). In 1996, a selection from his poems was translated into French and published in France in the series *Les cahiers de Royaumont* by Creaphis under the title *L'hiver est fini*. He has translated widely from English, American and Greek poets, and edited anthologies of verse translation. He has also published critical studies of Irish playwrights, including John Whiting, as well as translations of their plays.

MICHAEL HULSE has won the National Poetry Competition and the Bridport Poetry Competition (twice), has taken the Cholmondeley and other awards for his poetry, and co-edited the best-selling anthology *The New Poetry*. He is also widely praised as a translator from the German (W.G. Sebald, Elfriede Jelinek, Botho Strauss, Jakob Wassermann, Goethe), and has published criticism and lectured worldwide. The founder of the poetry press Leviathan, he recently established the new magazine *Leviathan Quarterly* after two and a half years co-editing *Stand* with John Kinsella. Michael Hulse is a former editor of the Arc international poetry series.

A. S. BYATT was educated at Cambridge, and was a senior lecturer in English at University College, London, before taking up writing full-time in 1983. Her novels include *Possession* (winner of the Booker Prize in 1990), and the sequence *The Virgin in the Garden, Still Life*, and *Babel Tower*. She has also written two novellas, published together as *Angels & Insects*, and four collections of shorter works, including *The Matisse Stories* and *The Djinn in the Nightingale's Eye*. As well as a novelist, she is also a distinguished critic.